Crucial Communication
Navigating Organizational Change with Confidence

Table of Contents

Chapter 1. Introduction

In today's dynamic business environment, one must stay steady in the face of constant change. Our Special Report, "Crucial Communication: Navigating Organizational Change with Confidence," is your guide to thriving amidst the inevitable flux. This engaging and practical resource provides vital strategies to spearhead change, master communication, and lead with assurance. Get ready to unlock the secrets of effective leadership, and experience the satisfying progression as your organization steps into the future with poise and purpose. Unlock the power to shape your organization positively by investing in this comprehensive report today. Let's jointly undertake this enlightening journey towards successful change management, one confident step at a time!

Chapter 2. Understanding the Dynamics of Change

Understanding the dynamics of change is synonymous to decoding the pulse of an organization's evolution. It is perceiving the patterns in chaos and turning potential disruption into opportunities for growth. It marries resilience with strategic insight to foster an enabling environment where transition becomes not just manageable, but profitable. To navigate this intricate labyrinth with assurance, one must comprehend certain key aspects of change – its nature, drivers, types, resistance, and management.

2.1. The Nature of Change

Change, by its very nature, is a constant in organizational life – an incessant ebb and flow of evolution. It represents moving from a known, current state to a less certain future state. Albeit often perceived as a threat, change should rather be viewed as an opportunity for improvement and growth. Its omnipresence, while unsettling at times, is imperative for organizations that intend to evolve in line with market trends and maintain their competitive edge in an increasingly demanding business landscape.

2.2. Drivers of Change

Change in an organization can stem from a multitude of factors:

1. Globalization: With the world becoming a closer-knitted village, the impacts of international politics, economics, and cultural shifts are more pronounced than ever.

2. Technological advancements: The escalation in technological innovation demands businesses to adapt continually to new and evolving methods and tools.

3. Regulatory changes: Legislation alterations and new guidelines oftentimes necessitate an organizational shift in practices and procedures.

4. Competitive pressures: The game of acquiring a greater market share keeps the business arena in constant dynamics, where change is the only way to stay ahead.

5. Internal factors: Changes in leadership, organizational culture, or business strategy may also catalyze organizational change.

Understanding these drivers is fundamental to steering your organization through the currents of change, leveraging these triggers as momentum, and channeling it towards growth and success.

2.3. Types of Change

It's critical to identify the type of change taking place since this classification aids in tailoring your strategy accordingly. Organizational changes can primarily fall under the following categories:

1. Strategic change: Changes in the overall direction of the organization.

2. Operational change: Changes in the way an organization works.

3. Technological change: Changes in the organization's equipment, software, or processes.

4. Cultural change: Changes in the shared values, norms, and behavior within the organization.

These categories aren't mutually exclusive and often overlap, making it vital for leaders to adopt a holistic perspective while managing organizational change.

2.4. Resistance to Change

Resistance is a natural response to change. It comes from a deep-rooted fear of the unknown, loss of control or comfort, perceived negative implications, or lack of understanding about the need and potential benefits of change. Identifying potential resistance and managing it is a critical aspect of the change management process.

"Overcoming Resistance to Change" is a topic that deserves a deep dive – and one that will be covered extensively in the following chapters.

2.5. Managing Change: An Overview

Change, executed correctly, can be a powerful tool for organizations. It can drive innovation, enhance efficiency, build stronger relationships amongst team members, and place an organization on a trajectory towards success. Change management takes a structured approach to ensure that changes are smoothly and successfully implemented, and that the benefits of these changes are achieved.

The organization's leadership must create a compelling case for change, design a vision and strategy, communicate it effectively to bring everyone onboard, implement the changes iteratively, and sustain it for long-term effectiveness. This, of course, constitutes a simplistic overview; effective change management is an elaborate dance involving several tactical moves, which will be discussed in-depth in the subsequent part of our report.

Navigating the dynamics of organizational change calls for an open mindset, deep understanding, meticulous planning, and astute execution. By understanding these dynamics of change, you have taken the first major stride towards transforming your organization's ability to thrive in the face of transition. The following sections will guide you further on this path of proactive transformation.

Remember, in the grand scheme of change, it's not the fittest, but the most adaptable that survive and thrive. It's about time that we embrace change as a constant companion in our organizational journey rather than perceiving it as an occasional visitor.

Chapter 3. The Role of Communication in Change Management

For any organization to successfully implement change, two things are critical: the change itself and how that change is communicated. Communication plays a central role in initiating, implementing, and reinforcing change. It is the link that connects all parts of an organization, making efficient and effective communication an imperative part of successful change management.

3.1. Elements of Effective Communication

Effective communication is not just about sharing information but about making sure that the information is understood, accepted, and acted upon. This involves several key elements such as clarity, consistency, and relevance.

1. **Clarity**: Clear and concise communication eliminates possible misunderstandings and uncertainty. When it comes to communicating change, clarify the why, what, and how of the change to alleviate any confusion or speculations among employees.

2. **Consistency**: Reinforce the key messages of the change consistently through multiple channels and styles to increase understanding and acceptance. Consistency is also critical in maintaining trust during times of change.

3. **Relevance**: Tailor the messaging to fit your audience's context and perspective. Providing relevant information to each group or individual will enable them to connect better with the change

and understand their role in it.

3.2. Communication Strategies for Change Management

A well-crafted communication strategy can mitigate several potential risks during change management. It helps minimize uncertainty, resistance to change, and misinterpretation of the change's intent and impact. Here are a few strategies for successful communication during change management:

1. **Start Early**: Start your communication effort as soon as the change decision is made. Doing so will prepare employees for the upcoming shift and reduce the shock when the change is officially introduced.

2. **Open Dialogue**: Encourage open discussions, queries, and suggestions. It not only builds trust but also helps uncover any root issues or concerns that may hamper the change process.

3. **Use Multiple Channels**: Leverage various channels to relay your message like emails, meetings, webinars, and internal social media. The objective is to ensure that everyone gets the message, irrespective of their preferred communication method.

4. **Repeat Your Message**: Repetition is key to remembering and understanding any new information. Reiterate your key change messages at regular intervals and through various platforms and channels.

3.3. Addressing Resistance with Communication

Resistance to change is natural. The unfamiliarity of new methods, processes, or systems can lead to discomfort and apprehension among employees. Communication can play a pivotal role in turning this resistance into acceptance and support.

Here are a few communication techniques that can be employed to manage resistance:

1. **Explain the Need for Change**: Be transparent about why the change is necessary. Detail out the pain points it is addressing and how it will benefit the organization in the long run.

2. **Offer Personal Benefits**: Employees are more likely to support change if they see a personal benefit. Communicate how the change will improve their work, knowledge, or career.

3. **Address Concerns Proactively**: Provide a platform where employees can voice their concerns without fear. Answer their questions honestly and sincerely to dispel any present and potential fears.

4. **Provide Regular Updates**: Keep everyone in the loop about the progress of the change. Regular reports about the status of the change can reduce anxiety, build trust, and foster a sense of involvement among employees.

3.4. Role of Leaders in Communication

Leadership is an essential component in change management, especially when it comes to communication. Leaders can act as role models, inspiring and motivating their team and mitigating resistance to change.

1. **Leader as an Enabler**: Leaders can foster an environment where open and honest communication is valued. By encouraging feedback and respecting differing opinions, leaders can make everyone in the organization a part of the change process.

2. **Leader as an Educator**: Leaders are often the ones who know the most about the necessity and benefits of the change. They can use their knowledge to educate their subordinates about the change, facilitating a deeper, more personal understanding of the change.

3. **Leader as an Influencer**: Through effective communication, leaders can influence their team members' perceptions of the change. By emphasizing the positive aspects of the change and addressing any concerns, they can shape the narrative of the change within their teams.

To sum up, the role of communication in change management cannot be understated. In essence, change is about people, and people are bound together by communication. So, mastering communication during change management will enable an organization to maintain cohesiveness, achieve employee buy-in, and ensure the successful realization of its intended changes.

Chapter 4. Building Confidence in the Face of Change

Change, despite being an inevitable and constant part of any organization's journey, is often met with resistance, uncertainty, and fear. This resistance stems primarily from the lack of confidence and trust in the process and outcome of change. Thus, building confidence in the face of change becomes a critical element in successful change management.

4.1. Why is Confidence Critical in Change Management?

Confidence is the assurance of our abilities to work towards meaningful outcomes even in uncertain circumstances. It serves as the key to successful adaptation and allows us to confront change with a positive mindset, ready to tackle all challenges head-on. By fostering confidence, we cultivate resilience, courage, and flexibility —traits necessary for not just surviving but thriving in the face of change.

For change initiatives to succeed, the confidence must be built at two levels. Firstly, the organization's leaders must possess confidence in their strategies and decisions. Secondly, this confidence needs to percolate down to the entire organization, inspiring trust and optimism among all employees. If either level lacks confidence, resistance replaces cooperation, questioning undermines execution, and the change initiative risks losing momentum or even failing entirely.

At its core, 'Confidence in Change Management' means instilling belief and trust in the planned interventions, the leadership directing them, and the overall success of the resulting transformation.

4.2. Strategies for Building Confidence

While it sounds challenging, building confidence for change is achievable with the right strategies:

1. **Transparency and Open Communication:** A clear, open communication line between the leadership and employees helps build trust. Make sure to convey what is changing, why it is changing, and how it impacts different teams. Let individuals ask questions, voice their concerns, and offer suggestions. This open dialogue fosters understanding, encourages participation, and builds confidence.

2. **Inclusion in the Change Process:** Including team members in the change process, decision-making, and strategy development fosters a sense of ownership and responsibility. This involvement enables individuals to tie in their contributions, building trust in the process, their abilities, and their resilience to changes.

3. **Effective Management of Achievements and Failures:** Cultivate a culture that recognizes and celebrates small wins as progress towards the bigger goal. This approach builds a progressive mindset and confidence in the direction of change. Conversely, also create a safe environment where mistakes can be learned from.

4. **Training and Skill Development:** Invest in enhancing employees' skills and capabilities to handle the new changes successfully. When employees are equipped to handle the demands of change, their confidence, adaptability, and acceptance of change improve.

5. **Consistent Leadership:** Stable, consistent leadership goes a long

way in instilling confidence. Leaders need to maintain a united front, continually expressing their belief in the change process, even though there might be disagreements behind the scenes. A confident and resilient leadership promotes a similar attitude throughout the organization.

4.3. Embodying Confidence as a Leader

The role of a leader in change management is pivotal. Leaders can boost employees' confidence through their actions, demeanor, and communication. They must display optimism, resilience, and confidence, even when faced with setbacks or resistance. By doing this, they effectively model the attitude they want to cultivate in their team.

Leaders could use various strategies to embody confidence:

1. **Emulating Confidence:** Leaders should set the example of embracing change with a positive attitude. This demonstration encourages employees to follow suit.

2. **Effective Communication:** Leaders should communicate efficiently about the necessity and benefits of change, the steps being taken to implement it, and the potential challenges ahead. Regular updates on progress can also bolster confidence in the journey.

3. **Inviting Participation:** Leaders should invite employees to take part in decision-making or project planning related to the change. This involvement fosters a sense of empowerment and confidence among employees.

4. **Providing Support:** Leaders should offer their support and be open to hearing any employee concerns. They should also provide resources for extra training or skill development that might be needed due to the changes.

4.4. Nurturing a Culture of Confidence

For lasting confidence, it is important to foster a work culture that encourages this trait. Invest in professional development and training, create a safe space for employees to voice their ideas and concerns, and reward those who take risks or show innovation. This shows employees that they are valued, that their voices and contributions matter, and ultimately builds their confidence in themselves and the organization.

Organizational change can be taxing and uncertain. Building confidence in the face of this change, therefore, forms an essential part of successful change management. Confidence at every level of the organization, from leadership to frontline employees, helps ensure acceptance, inspire participation, and reduce resistance to change. With the strategies shared in this chapter, you can overcome change resistance and successfully steer your organization through the seas of transformation.

Chapter 5. Leader's Guide to Navigating Organizational Shifts

In the realm of organizational leadership, accepting and navigating change is not just an option—it's a requirement. Even the most successful leaders can be challenged by the trials of transformation, but with the correct mindset and tools, they can effectively navigate their organizations through the uncertainties of transformation.

5.1. Understanding the Evolution

Executives, managers, and team leads must first understand the nature of change and its inherent intricacies. Change is a constant. Every organization, small or large, new or established, experiences change. Therefore, leaders must commit to continual learning, adaptability, and flexibility, instilling these attributes at the heart of their organizations.

Change often encounters resistance. As human beings, we are naturally protective of the status quo and are comfortable with familiarity, making us initially resistant to change. In an organizational context, this can translate to feelings of fear, anxiety, or insecurity among employees. Understanding this resistance and its root causes allows leaders to determine the correct approach to address these concerns and work towards acceptance and enthusiasm for the forthcoming changes.

5.2. Constructing the Change Narrative

Communicating change is a complex process but crafting a compelling, coherent, and transparent narrative around the necessary transformations is crucial. The narrative should clarify the organization's direction, the reasoning behind the change, and the benefits it will bring. The story should inspire employees and encourage them to take ownership in writing this new chapter in the organization's history.

The narrative is not simply a one-off speech or presentation but should be continually reinforced through continuous communication and symbolic action. To make sure your message is clear and adequately received, repeat it across multiple channels—company meetings, email updates, internal newsletters, and one-on-one meetings.

5.3. Building Trust through Transparency

Trust is the foundation of productive relationships, and in times of change, it becomes more important than ever. Transparency fosters trust. Leaders should, therefore, be open about the drivers of change, the intended outcomes, and potential hurdles. Even when messages are challenging or unfavorable, honesty reinforces trust, allowing leaders to maintain credibility and rapport with their teams.

Leaders also need to be transparent about their expectations. Role clarity, in terms of responsibilities and performance expectations during the change process, aids in lessening any confusion or apprehension among employees.

5.4. Facilitating Employee Engagement

Efficiently managing change involves more than pushing directives down the corporate ladder. Employees must feel they are a part of the process, contributing to solutions, and have their voices heard. Creating avenues for engagement such as workshops, town hall meetings, online forums or suggestion boxes, assists in acknowledging their concerns and gathering their valuable insights.

Leaders should encourage their teams to openly voice questions, worries, or suggestions to tap into the collective intelligence of their workforce. They should also remember to recognize and reward initiatives and foster an environment where new ideas aligned with the change are appreciated.

5.5. Handling Resistance

When the shift gets hard, resistance rolls in. A crucial part of managing change is therefore managing resistance. Understanding the reasons behind resistance—whether it stems from fear of the unknown, perceived loss of control, or concerns over job security—helps in designing effective strategies to counteract it.

Acknowledging resistance rather than ignoring it, and empathizing with those having difficulty adjusting to change can smooth the transition. Regular communication, offering support, and providing training when necessary can also assist in easing the process.

5.6. Cultivating Resilience

Organizational change can spark turbulence, and leaders must be ready to tackle this head-on. Building resilience—both on a personal level and within their teams—is crucial in ensuring the capacity to endure uncertainty, recover from setbacks, and adapt positively to change.

Leaders can nurture resilience by promoting a positive and supportive company culture, providing resources and training to cope with change, and celebrating successes, no matter how small, during the transition period.

Navigating the waters of organizational change may seem daunting, but with the right mindset, tools, and understanding, leaders can chart a course that not only successfully manages the change but turns it into an opportunity for growth and innovation. For when we are willing to embrace change and drive it forward with confidence, we are truly able to unlock the vast potential that lies within both ourselves and our organizations.

Chapter 6. Driving Change: Proactive Vs Reactive Strategies

To navigate shifts in the business landscape, it's critical to understand that change can be approached in two basic ways: proactively or reactively. This delineation forms the framework for crafting strategies, serving as touchstones amidst the turbulence of transformation.

6.1. Rooted in Circumstances: A Look at Proactive and Reactive Change

Change is inherent to all businesses. But the motives and mechanisms that instigate this change can be as diverse as the businesses themselves. Distinguishingly, proactive change is ignited by foresight and strategic decision making, while reactive change is driven by sudden external factors.

Proactive change is born out of a high level of preparedness and forward-thinking. It is when an organization seeks to instigate change from a place of strategic planning, rather than as a response to external forces. This may involve, for example, embracing new technologies, innovating product lines, or entering new markets to seize emerging opportunities or avert potential threats.

On the other hand, reactive change occurs when an organization must adapt quickly to changes in the environment. This could be reacting to regulatory shifts, market disruptions, competitor strategies, or internal crises. It's about surviving and then thriving in unplanned, unexpected situations.

Understanding where your strategy falls on this spectrum can help you gut-check your readiness for change and adapt appropriately.

6.2. Crafting Proactive Change: A Panoramic View

Anticipating change isn't just a prescient power held by oracle-like CEOs, it's a capability that can be developed through strategic foresight, environmental scanning, and scenario planning.

Strategic foresight involves looking ahead to identify possible future developments, while environmental scanning is about keeping a vigilant eye on socio-economic, technological, and political landscapes for potential change catalysts. Scenario planning then uses these insights to create different future scenarios and develop strategies.

Through this scanning-and-scenario mode, businesses can stay prepared for inevitable flux and lead from a place of strength rather than scrambling to respond when change hits.

Thus, proactive change starts with investing in knowledge gathering systems. Then, it proceeds to hone the ability to filter through this knowledge and spot significant signals. Finally, it demands the development of flexible strategies and structures that can respond swiftly to encountered changes.

6.3. Reactive Change: An Act of Resilience

Reactive change is not inferior to proactive change. Rather, it tests an organization's resilience and nimbleness. Unexpected changes can still be overcome with strategic decision-making despite the pressing need for immediate action. The key lies in being prepared to pivot when necessary and cultivating a culture that promotes rapid response and adaptation.

Emphasis should be placed on establishing crisis management protocols. These should clearly outline the roles, responsibilities, and decision-making processes in the event of sudden change. Training the team in crisis management will further enhance an organization's reactive capacities.

Beyond managing crisis, it's important to cultivate an environment of constant learning and adaptation. Encourage teams to experiment, to fail fast, learn fast, and adjust course accordingly. Be it embracing remote work during a pandemic or repurposing infrastructure to meet new demands, an organization's survival and growth often hinge on its ability to react to changes quickly and effectively.

6.4. Striking the Balance: Integrating Proactive and Reactive Strategies

Resilience is a fine dance between anticipation and reaction. An organization must not only track and confront emerging trends but also adjust and respond when unexpected changes occur. Therefore, the most effective change management strategies combine proactive and reactive approaches.

For instance, a company might routinely monitor changes in technology and competitive landscapes (proactive) while also preparing for unforeseen disruptions through contingency planning (reactive). In this way, the proactive strategy forms the backdrop, but the reactive ability is also in place if needed.

6.5. Mastering the Double-Edged Sword of Change

Change can be a challenging beast to navigate. This chapter has exposed two major strategies to use when steering the ship of change: proactive and reactive. Both entail different requirements and yield varying results depending on the circumstances.

Remember, effectively driving change is not about picking one strategy over another. Instead, it's about understanding the dynamics of your environment and then adopting a balanced approach. In the end, it is the organizations that are flexible enough to anticipate change, yet strong enough to absorb the blows of unanticipated shocks, that emerge victorious in the ever-evolving marketplace.

Chapter 7. The Art of Persuasion: Convincing Others to Embrace Change

Efficient leadership, especially during periods of significant transition, entails not only the ability to innovate and adapt but also the prowess to inspire your team to hop on the change journey. The linchpin to initiating successful change often lies in the aptitude to persuade. Being persuasive isn't about manipulation or coercion, but it's about presenting a vision so convincing that others willingly come on board. Let's delve deep into the various facets of this powerful technique.

7.1. Understanding the Power of Persuasion

Persuasion is an essential part of our everyday lives. From advertisements that influence our buying choices to practicing diplomatic tact in negotiations, it permeates every aspect of our professional and personal lives. Specifically in terms of organizational change, persuasion is the beacon of light that makes employees forego their comfort zones and embrace what could be a path fraught with uncertainty. Understanding that the change being proposed would be beneficial in the long run, and communicating this convincingly, is what will drive people towards accepting it.

7.2. Building a Convincive Case for Change

First and foremost, there needs to be a convincing reason why the proposed change is necessary. This isn't the time for vague assertions or nebulous promises. Leaders must present clear, specific, and fact-based reasons why the change is not only inevitable, but beneficial. Never underestimate the potency of concrete information and reliable data.

It's essential to craft a compelling story that weaves together your vision, the need for change, and the future benefits that will be reaped. A story not only catches attention, but it also connects on an emotional level, enabling your team to visualize and internalize the intended transformation. The more vivid your vision, the more incentivized your team would be to partake in it.

7.3. Connecting with People's Needs and Emotions

A rudimentary mistake leaders make is to assume that a demonstrably advantageous scenario will automatically convince others to accept change. However, people aren't purely rational beings. Our decisions are often intertwined with emotions and deeply-held beliefs. Therefore, a successful persuasive push should also engage at an emotional level.

You should perceive change from your team's perspective – what are their fears, anxieties, and reservations? Establishing an emotional connection, addressing these concerns, and affirming your commitment to support them through the transition, will secure their trust and motivation.

7.4. Communication: The Key to Persuasion

Persuasion, fundamentally, is an act of communication. But, effective communication goes beyond mere transmission of information. It involves listening, empathy, and an open dialogue that promotes understanding and alignment of viewpoints.

Transparent and timely communication curtails uncertainty and speculation, initiating a positive discourse around the proposed transformation. Remember to court feedback with grace. It not only lends you critical insight into general sentiment but also makes employees feel valued and included in the change process.

7.5. Demonstrating Credibility and Authority

Your persuasive efforts would be futile if you're not viewed as credible. That's why leaders need to embody the change they're communicating. If you're championing a culture of innovation, show that you're an innovator too. If you're calling for increased collaboration, demonstrate your willingness to foster teamwork.

Credibility also stems from consistency. If your message varies, it breeds doubt and resistance. Ensure your verbal and non-verbal communication align with the vibrant image of change you're presenting.

7.6. Mastering the Art of Influence

Mastering the art of persuasion necessitates mastering the art of influence. Influential leaders foster strong relationships, are attentive and responsive, and inspire trust and loyalty. By leveraging your influence, you can win ardent advocates for your cause, making your change movement an unstoppable force.

7.7. Inclusion: Key to Reducing Resistance

Resistance to change is natural, but inclusion can soften it substantially. By involving people in the decision-making process, you're not only reducing 'change as a threat' perception but also getting essential perspectives that may strengthen your change plan.

7.8. Implementing Change Gradually

Abrupt alterations can often incite panic and resistance. Using a phased approach not only facilitates smooth transitions but also allows for valuable learning to be incorporated along the way.

Persuasion is a potent leadership tool when wields properly. Through the judicious use of persuasion, you can rally your team behind your vision of change, ensuring a seamless transition and future growth. Embrace the art of persuasion and become the transformative leader your organization needs.

Chapter 8. Crafting Comprehensive Change Communications

Change is a constant feature of any thriving organization, and the key to successfully navigating this change lies in comprehensive and clear communication. Proper planning, concise messaging, involvement of key stakeholders and consistent application of these strategies can enable an organization to thrive in the wake of change.

8.1. The Importance of Effective Communication during Change

People respond to change in different ways - some adapt easily while others resist or deny its existence until it's too late. Effective communication caters to the varied reactions, explaining why the change is essential and how it will positively affect the organization and its members.

While this may seem like an overwhelming task, breaking it down into components simplifies the process. These components are Transparency, Clarity, Dialog, and Consistency.

8.1.1. Transparency

People appreciate honesty; transparency builds trust, an essential element during a transition. It ensures accurate information is relayed, reducing the chance of false rumors spreading. This promotes a sense of security amongst employees, reducing resistance to change.

8.1.2. Clarity

Clear communication implies detailed and straightforward messaging. Avoid jargon and business-speak. Use simple language to explain: why the change is necessary, its advantages, how it will be implemented, what role each will play, and how it will affect them.

8.1.3. Dialog

Encourage interaction. Employees should feel comfortable raising questions or concerns without fear of backlash. This promotes an open environment and encourages participation in the change process.

8.1.4. Consistency

Keep the communication consistent - in the chosen channels, frequency and messaging. This not only keeps everyone informed and updated but also helps in retaining the faith and confidence in the organization.

8.2. Planning and Implementing Effective Change Communication Strategies

Proper planning is of utmost importance when laying the groundwork for change communication. Let's look at how this can be implemented:

8.2.1. Define Objectives

Start by clearly defining the objectives of the change. These goals should align with the overall strategic direction of the organization and should be easily communicated to all stakeholders.

8.2.2. Identify Stakeholders

Note down all possible people who will be affected by this change. This is your primary communication audience, and their understanding and acceptance of the change are crucial.

8.2.3. Designate a Change Leadership Team

Create a dedicated team responsible for managing and communicating the change. This team should consist of members from different functional areas within the organization for a more wholesome perspective.

8.2.4. Create a Communication Plan

Outline a robust communication plan detailing what will be communicated, when, how, and to whom. This plan should include a tactical roadmap for timely and efficient communication.

8.2.5. Implement, Review, and Adapt

Once the plan is in place, commence implementation. It is essential to continuously monitor the process, review the effectiveness of the communication, and adapt as required.

8.3. Handling Resistance to Change

Resistance is a typical response to change. It represents fear or uncertainty of the unknown. Recognizing and effectively managing resistance are crucial steps towards successful change management.

8.3.1. Open Dialogues

Open dialogues about fears and uncertainties. This will not only help alleviate anxiety but also gives you insight into potential challenges from an employee perspective.

8.3.2. Empathy and Support

Show empathy towards people's concerns. Provide them with the necessary support. This will strengthen their trust in the decision-makers, thereby reducing resistance.

8.3.3. Training and Guiding

Provide relevant training to support employees through the change. Also, guide them on how to adapt effectively, thereby accelerating the transition process and making it smoother.

8.4. Communication Channel Selection

The choice of communication channels is just as vital as the message. The mediums used should be appropriate to the complexity and impact of the change. Multi-channel communication usually works the best – providing the opportunity to adapt the messaging based on the recipients and the content.

Change is inevitable, but with the right tools, it needn't be daunting. At the heart of these tools lies communication. A carefully crafted org-wide message instills confidence, clarifies doubts, and helps guide everyone in the right direction - ensuring a smoother transition and a better future for all stakeholders.

Chapter 9. Overcoming Resistance and Conflicts: A Practical Approach

Change is inevitable, but it is not always welcomed, particularly within established organizations. Resistance to change, often rooted in fear and uncertainty, can fuel conflict and hamper progress. As a leader, it's your duty to anticipate and address this resistance head-on. In doing so, you stand to encourage productivity, improve morale, and foster a culture of adaptivity within your team.

9.1. Understanding Resistance

First and foremost, it's crucial to understand the root causes behind resistance to change. By doing so, you can more effectively address and neutralize it. Resistance can stem from a multitude of factors, including but not limited to: fear of the unknown, loss of control, perceived threats to job security, and lack of trust in leadership. Personal attitudes, institutional culture, and previous experiences with unsuccessful changes can also contribute to resistance.

Understanding resistance is an ongoing process, not a one-time event. Encourage open dialogue about anxieties related to upcoming changes. Learn about your team's past experiences with change, and use this insight to inform your strategies.

9.2. The Role of Effective Communication in Overcoming Resistance

Communication is essential in overcoming resistance to change.

People fear what they don't understand, so clear, consistent, and honest communication can help put their minds at ease.

Share as much information as possible about the upcoming changes, including the reasons behind them, the expected timeline, and how they will affect individual team members. Understand that change often implies uncertainty, and be ready to answer questions and address concerns as they arise.

9.3. Encouraging Participation and Involvement

Smooth transition into new phases comes from participation and involvement. Encourage team members to voice their thoughts and contribute their ideas regarding the change. By involving them in the process, you convey respect for their opinions, which can help to build trust and mitigate resistance.

9.4. Identifying and Addressing Sources of Conflict

Conflict can be a byproduct of resistance to change. It's imperative to identify potential sources of conflict early and address them proactively. This might require mediation or conflict management interventions. Moreover, developing strategies for managing conflict can be very beneficial. These might include creating open channels for dialogue and feedback, fostering a culture that values differing opinions and constructive criticism, and implementing well-defined procedures for resolving conflicts.

9.5. Empathize and Support

Change often means stepping out of your comfort zone, which can prove daunting for many. As a leader, it's important to empathize with these feelings and provide support to your team members. This looks different depending on your organization and the individuals involved, but may include counseling services, providing extra training or resources, or simply being available to listen when someone needs to talk.

9.6. Reinforcement and Rewards

Lastly, positive reinforcement and rewards can be very effective at reducing resistance. The team members who adapt quickly and show a positive attitude towards change should be recognized and rewarded. This not only encourages them to continue doing so but can also incentivize others to adopt a similar attitude.

Overcoming resistance and conflicts requires a strategic and empathetic approach. As leaders, we must not only calculate the necessary structural adjustments but also understand and navigate the human reaction to these changes. By being open to the fears and concerns of your team, communicating frequently and effectively, and encouraging involvement in the change process, you'll be able to lead your organization confidently through any upheaval. And in doing so, you will set a strong foundation for a future-focused organization that is resilient in the face of change and prepared to seize whatever opportunities the future may hold.

Chapter 10. Post-implementation: Evaluating and Sustaining the Change

Executing a change within an organization is a feat of immense challenge, but it is only half the journey. The latter half, and equally important, entails maintaining the implemented change, evaluating its effectiveness, and ensuring its sustainability over the long haul. Without thorough dedication to these aspects, even the most well-planned change can fizzle out or fall by the wayside.

10.1. Evaluating the Change

In today's fast-paced business environment, change is not an isolated event but an ongoing process. Once a change gets implemented, it is essential to gauge its efficiency and success. Regular evaluations can provide vital insights into how the change is affecting the organization and whether it is delivering the expected outcomes. For a successful evaluation, you must establish proper metrics and tools.

Key Performance Indicators: KPIs serve as quantifiable measures that can quantify success. These indicators should correlate with the desired outcomes of the change.

Surveys and Feedback: Employee feedback can give crucial insights into how well the change is received and its impact on staff morale, productivity, and satisfaction.

Quantitative Measurements: Financial aspects like profits, return on investment, and sales figures can illustrate the change's financial impact.

An evaluation should not only focus on the outcomes but also on the process itself. It can highlight the strategies that worked well and those that require improvement, thereby framing the approach for future change initiatives.

10.2. Sustaining the Change

Sustaining the implemented change is a critical follow-up to the evaluation process. Without adequate maintenance, there can be a regress to old habits and patterns, nullifying the effort put into initiating the change. Some key strategies to sustain change include:

Reinforcement: Employees should regularly revisit the reasons behind the change and the benefits it has brought. Regular reinforcement sessions can serve as a recall and encourage them to adhere to the new process.

Rewards and Recognition: Recognizing and rewarding those who demonstrate successful adoption of the change can motivate others to do the same.

Refresher Training: Training sessions can assist employees in understanding and adapting to the new rules and processes.

10.3. Embedding Change into Organizational Culture

Organizational culture is a potent force that can support or hinder change initiatives. Integrating the change into the organization's culture can create an environment that fosters adjustment and discourages regression to old ways. A few pointers to achieve this are:

Moulding Beliefs and Values: Highlight the benefits and value of the change to the employees to instil belief. With strong conviction in the change, acceptance becomes second nature.

Role Modelling: Leaders should showcase the desired behaviours that align with the change initiative. Their actions can set a precedent for the employees to follow.

Establishing Change as a Norm: Awareness that change is a constant necessity and part of the organization's growth can play a crucial role in fostering resilience and adaptability among employees.

10.4. The Continued Role of Leadership

Leadership doesn't end with the successful implementation of change. Leaders must encourage feedback, open discussions, and continue to communicate, ensuring the change stays effective and the positives of the change are continuously highlighted.

10.5. Developing a Learning Organization

Continually learning and adapting are keys to longevity and success. Organizations that promote a learning culture tend to be more flexible and better equipped to handle change. Encouraging an environment of mutual learning and knowledge sharing can make the organization resilient and dynamic, ready to face any changes that the future might hold.

As we conclude, it is essential to reiterate that carrying out a change successfully is just the start. Ensuring it is effective, sustained, and ingrained into the very essence of your organization's culture, is what ensures the longevity and success of the change. As your organization continues to embrace change, remember - adaptation is not an end-destination but a journey.

Chapter 11. Case Studies: Successful Change Navigation Stories

In the vast expanse of organizational change, many robust and successful stories offer insight and practical strategies for navigating change. These stories offer tangible proof of the power of effective change management and the transformations it can bring to an organization.

11.1. The Shift of Microsoft

Perhaps one of the well-known examples of successful change navigation is the transformation of Microsoft under the leadership of Satya Nadella. In 2014, Nadella became CEO after the company had faced significant challenges, including a stagnant stock price and lack of innovation compared to competitors. Nadella knew he had to invoke rapid change to revitalize the tech giant.

Nadella's strategy revolved around the concept of a "growth mindset," a concept taken from psychology that focuses on learning from failure and continuous improvement. This idea was revolutionary for Microsoft, as the organization had a cluttered history of blaming and avoiding failure. Under Nadella's leadership, Microsoft moved towards accepting failures as opportunities for learning, embracing risk-taking, and fostering innovation.

Effective change communication played a vital role throughout this transformation. Nadella used town hall meetings, annual leadership conferences, and the company intranet to reiterate the new course. He also took steps to ensure the change happened at every level of the organization. Direct reports were encouraged to adopt the growth mindset, which gradually influenced various layers of

Microsoft.

The result? Microsoft re-emerged as a leading innovator, developed successful new products, and saw its stock price triple in just a few years. More importantly, the company culture transformed, leading to staggering improvements in employee satisfaction and engagement.

11.2. The Digital Transformation of Walmart

In the retail industry, the change story of Walmart is inspiring. As the largest physical retailer globally, Walmart found itself lagging in the rapidly growing e-commerce market dominated by Amazon. The need for change was apparent, and Doug McMillon, CEO since 2014, led the company on an ambitious path of digital transformation with the goal to seamlessly integrate online and offline channels.

McMillon introduced a restructuring plan which included investing heavily in e-commerce, acquiring smaller online retailers, and improving website and mobile apps to enhance the customer experience. Crucial to this change management strategy was communication within the company, involving every employee in the strategic vision.

Walmart instituted rigorous training programs, keeping employees abreast of the ongoing changes and equipping them with new skill sets. McMillon also placed a strong emphasis on transforming the organizational culture to align with the digital era, focusing on agility, innovation, and customer-centricity.

By executing this change strategy, Walmart managed to pivot successfully, registering rapid e-commerce growth, and significantly boosting its competitiveness against e-commerce giants.

11.3. The Revival of IBM

IBM's transformation under CEO Lou Gerstner is a classic example of how a company facing downfall can turn around with effective change management. When Gerstner took over in 1993, IBM was on the brink of bankruptcy after years of struggling to adapt to the rapidly evolving tech landscape.

Gerstner's transformation strategy was bold and unexpected—he decided IBM would stop selling individual technology components and instead offer integrated technology solutions. This new business model required drastic changes ranging from reconfiguring the company's operations to transforming its organizational culture.

To bring about this immense change, Gerstner communicated a clear and consistent vision of integrated solutions. He also initiated a cultural shift towards focusing on customers rather than products, encouraging employees to think in terms of solutions rather than individual components.

This remarkable change was a success. IBM regained its position as a leading technology company and, more importantly, established a robust change-ready culture that continues to adapt to evolving business landscapes.

11.4. The Reinvention of Adobe

Lastly, the story of Adobe's transformation from a traditional software vendor into a leading cloud-based service provider stands out. Sailing in the troubled waters of stagnating profits and a sluggish stock price, Adobe realized the need for drastic changes to survive.

Under CEO Shantanu Narayen, Adobe undertook an aggressive shift towards the subscription-based model. The idea was to replace the high-cost, one-time fee with a lower, monthly subscription price, thereby providing continuous value to customers and recurring revenue to the company.

The change was tough, as it required customers to adapt to a new pricing model and employees to adjust to selling and supporting subscription products. Narayen facilitated this change with clear and continuous communication, regularly updating sales teams on revenue goals and educating customers about the benefits of the new model.

Adobe's transformation was a massive success. The move to a subscription-based model resulted in significant recurring revenues, soaring stock prices, and high customer satisfaction. It displayed how effective change management, combined with a clear vision and strategic communication, can reinvent a company and secure its future.

In conclusion, these case studies are powerful reminders of how change, when managed efficiently and communicated effectively, can help organizations adapt, grow, and prosper. Understanding and learning from these successful change navigation stories can empower leaders to confidently navigate through their own journey of organizational change.